Emperor Maximilian I of Mexico: The Life of the Last European Monarch in Mexico

By Gustavo Vázquez Lozano & Charles River Editors

Portrait of the emperor circa 1864

About Charles River Editors

Charles River Editors provides superior editing and original writing services across the digital publishing industry, with the expertise to create digital content for publishers across a vast range of subject matter. In addition to providing original digital content for third party publishers, we also republish civilization's greatest literary works, bringing them to new generations of readers via ebooks.

Sign up here to receive updates about free books as we publish them, and visit Our Kindle Author Page to browse today's free promotions and our most recently published Kindle titles.

Introduction

Charlotte, the emperor's wife

Emperor Maximilian I of Mexico

   Once upon a time, when a Civil War threatened to fracture the US, there was a monarchy south of the Rio Grande. That kingdom was called Mexico. It had a magnificent castle, a beautiful princess and a tall, handsome prince; he was noble and idealistic, he had fire in his heart, but he was weak and gullible. A fool, some would say. One day, when he was still a teenager, he wrote, "Ambition is like the balloonist. To some extent, the rise is nice and he does enjoy a splendid view and a vast landscape. But when he rises more, vertigo occurs, the air becomes thin and the risk of a big fall increases." With this parable, the Austrian Archduke Maximilian of Hapsburg inadvertently predicted the destiny to which he would bravely ride, despite the warnings and the sweet talkers. In any case, he followed his heart´s mandate. And Charlotte, the princess, was "one of the most cultured and beautiful" in Europe. Since she was a girl she'd known that one day she would become a queen or an empress.

When it was first hinted that they would be offered the crown of Mexico, she was 22 and he was 28, and they were surrounded by the intrigue and ambition of their own brothers, who could not wait to have them removed from the picture. So when, three years later, the couple received the official diplomatic mission which affirmed Mexico required their presence, the proposition was like a fairy tale come true. In the imagination of the era, Mexico was the distant paradise described by the great geographer Alexander von Humboldt: thick jungles and forests, steaming volcanoes, copious gold and silver mines, infinite beaches and exotic birds. "The most dangerous worldview is the worldview of those who have not viewed the world," the Prussian explorer had written, and Max believed it in all sincerity and contemplated the adventure with the eyes of his soul.

In Mexico, the reality was different from the imagination. It was too late by the time they realized they had been seduced by sirens, specifically the siren sitting upon the throne of France, Napoleon III. The zealous emperor frowned at the expansion of the US and the Protestant, Anglo-Saxon race. But there were also the vast territories of northern Mexico to consider, the gold and silver mines, plus Napoleon's vague idea of rebuilding the Latin race and culture in the Americas. With that in mind, he brought two puppets to his global stage, Maximilian and Charlotte, and made sure they were told that the Mexican people would tender unto them a carpet of roses as soon as they saw their royal feet touch their land. In their dreams, Max of Austria and Charlotte of Belgium would become the saviors of the ancient empire of Montezuma, now unable to govern itself, and on the road to self-destruction. But Maximilian was not thinking of conquest and looting, as did his ancestor, Charles I of Spain, but in reconstruction and healing. It is not that he was guilty of arrogance, either. Sending a European monarch to the American continent sounds outrageous these days, but at the time, it was common for the kings of England, Belgium, Greece or Bulgaria to be of other nationalities. Still, Maximilian refused to accept the throne of Mexico until he was shown evidence that the Mexicans agreed. When he was shown a pretend plebiscite, he agreed on the dangerous adventure.

The tragedy of Maximilian and Charlotte was romantic and political. In Mexico's official history, the one recorded by the winners, they were an affront to independence and a symbol of European arrogance. For the monarchies of Europe, they are a sad and embarrassing memory, because of the abandonment, craftiness and treachery they lived through. Repentance came too late, as both were dead by then. One was buried in his grave, and the other had been driven insane. It's something that might have been penned by Shakespeare himself. Their story has been told many times, not only by historians, but also by filmmakers, novelists, and dramaturges. It all happened 150 years ago, but Mexicans—both inside and outside the country—still remember the lights and shadows of that time. Some look at the timeworn photographs with respect and sadness; others, with contempt. "The old nations have the disease of memories," Maximilian wrote, and Mexico, the country that he and his wife loved until their last breath, is already showing signs of aging.

Emperor Maximilian I of Mexico: The Life of the Last European Monarch in Mexico chronicles the tumultuous life and reign of the last European ruler in Mexico. Along with pictures of important people, places, and events, you will learn about Emperor Maximilian like never before, in no time at all.

Emperor Maximilian I of Mexico: The Life of the Last European Monarch in Mexico

About Charles River Editors

Introduction

Ayala Anguiano, Armando, (2005). La epopeya de México, Tomo II. De Juárez al PRI. México: Fondo de Cultura Económica.

Del Paso, Fernando (2009). *News from the Empire*. USA: Dalkey Archive Press

Hamnet, Brian (1994). *Juárez*. Essex, England: Longman.

Pani, Erika, (2004). *El Segundo Imperio*. México: Fondo de Cultura Económica-CIDE.

Chapter 1: Mexico in Chaos

Every story has a time and place. The time for this story is the second half of the nineteenth century, the setting, Mexico, a "new" country, at least when compared with European kingdoms. After 300 years it had won its independence from Spain, but more than a real nation, Mexico was only a huge territory, populated in the center and almost deserted in its northern states; most of its original indigenous population had withdrawn to the impenetrable southern jungles. The political, economic, and cultural life took place in Mexico City, where once had stood splendid Tenochtitlan, the throne of Montezuma. There was some life in central Mexico, the cities of Veracruz, Puebla, Guadalajara, and in a few mining towns.

But beyond the magnificent Mexico City, not much happened in the rest of the country, except for the exploitation of natural resources, especially minerals from the north and south that were shipped to the capital. And war; there was war all the time. The constant military revolts and coups disturbed the economy and public finances, but especially the people, already tired of power struggles and revolutions. Between 1821 and Maximilian's arrival, there was not a single president of Mexico who could finish his term peacefully. With the notable exception of Guadalupe Victoria (the first president), every other head of state was ousted by an uprising or a coup. Between 1823 and 1864 Mexico changed its president 57 times, and never peacefully. [i] In comparison, the United States had only twelve presidents in the same period. This can give us a good idea of how unstable the country really was.

Although the Mexican government's budget was meager and sometimes nonexistent, there wasn't a single president who was able to rule in peace without having to commit the country's scarce resources to quell rebellions and uprisings. Industry, commerce, and the arts barely survived. The rural population suffered the torment of the cam, the forced recruiting of peasants by the insubordinate general of the day. It was actually a miracle that the country did not disintegrate. At the risk of oversimplification, the cause of all this instability and violence was the struggle between two parties or ideological positions, the "conservatives" versus the "liberals." Sometimes luck favored one side, sometimes the other. There were times when Mexico had two governments in different cities.

The political ruckus and consequent inattention of the vast northern and southern territories cost the country the loss of large areas. Central America, which once formed part of Mexico, was lost first. Twenty years later, Texas seceded. When it did, the state was populated more by white Protestant Americans than Mexicans. Three years later, the United States snatched half of the territory that still remained (the current states of Arizona, California, Colorado, Nevada, New Mexico, Utah and Wyoming) after a war between a disorganized, chaotic, and defenseless country against a powerful, opportunistic, and expanding US. Mexico could have lost even more (the Baja California Peninsula, Chiapas, and Yucatan) but the obstinacy of its statesmen, and a little luck, set its definite boundaries in 1854.

The country's misfortunes did not end there. Three years later a new and very violent war broke out between the Conservatives and the Liberals. Thirty-six years of independence from Spain had passed, and the country had apparently made a big mistake. The economy was bankrupt, Mexico had lost more than half of its territory, and external debt went from 34 to 64 million pesos and was impossible to pay. Even worse, the money had not been used to create infrastructure, but to finance revolutions. Mexico, many thought, was unable to govern itself.

A few powers—the United States included—hovered like vultures over the troubled country, hoping to take the spoils of its immense natural resources. Both Conservatives and Liberals, in order to get money and military support, did not hesitate to offer the country, in part or in whole, to foreign powers. In 1862, when Mexico declared a debt moratorium, the governments of Spain, France, and England threatened with military action. To be more persuasive, they sent warships to Veracruz, a port on the Gulf of Mexico. It was in this context that some of the so-called conservatives reasoned that Mexico's salvation depended on something that seemed hopeless: to ask a European power to help establish a monarchy, and a strong government that could provide stability and unity. A crowned head could rescue the country from collapse. Without it, the country was destined to implode, and it would happen soon. "We are lost if Europe does not come to our aid," wrote Lucas Alamán, one of the most respected and intelligent members of the Conservative Party.

Alamán

Mexico took a breather when, thanks to diplomatic work, the fleets of Spain and England withdrew from its shores. However, Napoleon III made it clear that his intentions went beyond simple debt collection. France had inflated its claims to absurd levels. Taking advantage of internal problems in the United States, then amidst its Civil War, the emperor saw the opportunity to extend France's presence in Latin American and slow American expansionism.[ii] It would be Napoleon's "most glorious enterprise." The Mexican Conservative Party and some crowned heads in Europe had already laid eyes on newlyweds Maximilian and Charlotte—both determined, intelligent and idealistic—for the crown of Mexico. The pieces were in place, but the throne of Montezuma had to be conquered first, like Spaniard Hernán Cortes had done in the sixteenth century. Only nobody had asked the Mexicans what they thought about it.

Napoleon III

Chapter 2: Maximilian and Charlotte

Maximilian at the age of 20

Maximilian of Habsburg was born in 1832 in Austria. His parents were named Franz Karl and Sophie, and he had an older brother named Franz Joseph, who at 18 became Emperor of Austria and King of Hungary, Croatia, and Bohemia, a position he held for 70 years. Since childhood, Maximilian was distinguished by his intelligence, his love for the arts, and his people skills. He could speak German, English, French, Czech, Hungarian, and Italian. Later he learned Spanish, and expressed his wish to learn the Nahuatl indigenous language, as a large number of people still spoke it in Mexico at the time. His education was comprised of several disciplines, including military science, international politics, and diplomacy. He was handsome, intellectual, and had a charming personality.

His mother considered him to be her most compassionate child. He was noble and sensitive, and was as interested in gardening as in poetry. "In family presentations he captivated his relatives with his theatrical and comic interpretations. Maximilian stood out as the handsome, hearty and much livelier brother. The young prince immersed himself in a variety of subjects, passionately longing for great adventures around the world." (McAllen, 2015).

When he was 19, his family sent him to different countries in Europe to meet his cousins. At that time, his brother, Franz Joseph, had ascended the throne of Austria, and Maximilian told him his desire to become a naval officer. Although Max's temperament was more of an academic, he was promoted to admiral and commander of the army, not by his influence, but thanks to his energetic and courageous service, which even his political rivals acknowledged.

Franz Joseph

One afternoon during his days as a sailor, they were surprised by a particularly violent storm and sought shelter in the Gulf of Trieste, Italy. There he saw a rocky ledge above the sea. Max became fascinated with that landscape, and it was there, on that same rock, where he later built his dream castle of Miramar. In 1856, he visited Napoleon III, the Emperor of the French, with whom he had a friendship; from there he went to Belgium.

In Brussels he had a meeting that would define his destiny. It was there he met Charlotte Amélie, one of the most intelligent, beautiful, and wealthy princesses of Europe, the daughter of King Leopold of Belgium. He became immediately attracted to the beautiful and intelligent girl of 16, with whom he shared a number of interests.

When she was a young child, Charlotte's mother fell ill with tuberculosis. The disease afflicted her for many, long years, and her daughter had to watch her slowly die. The grieving father tried to get closer to his children, Charlotte and her two ambitious brothers. The older brother, the future King Leopold II of Belgium, tried to appropriate some of her goods through dubious schemes, but King Leopold loved his daughter very much and obstructed his son's ploys. The king gave his three children the same education, meaning that Charlotte received an education considered to be "masculine" at the time, and which included philosophy, science, and politics. She absorbed everything easily, having inherited her father's intelligence and strong character (Ratz, 2008). At thirteen, she was already learning about how a kingdom's administration should be run. She even used to attend State meetings with his father, where matters of diplomacy and politics were frequently discussed.

Leopold II

When she met Maximilian, Charlotte was one of the most cultured and beautiful princesses in Europe, and one of the richest heiresses. She spoke French, German, Flemish, and English, and was an avid reader. "Slender with a small nose and sharp eyes, which seemed to communicate her ever-present thoughts and moods, she kept her thick brown hair in braids encircling her head.

Although she could be light-hearted, she preferred the seriousness of matters of state. Her composure was sometimes mistaken for vanity." Their wedding took place in 1857, when the future empress of Mexico was seventeen. The next day, "in a tearful state over leaving her father, but happy, [she] said goodbye at her mother's grave and to her lifelong home" (McAllen, 2015).

The couple wed in the princess's hometown, but they did not move immediately to Miramare Castle, since it was still under construction. Maximilian was very interested in the whole process; he relied on his style and taste for designs, and had extravagant gardens planted with trees he had collected from around the world. He filled the interiors with pictures of his ancestors and relatives. Charlotte, who was a good artist, contributed with some paintings, too.

The couple

Miramare Castle

For a time, Maximilian took over the government of Lombardy-Venetia, but he was never well-accepted by the people, and despite his good intentions, his brother vetoed almost all his projects. Soon, Austria lost that territory, and Maximilian was left with nothing to rule over. The young couple, looking for a political mission, was disheartened. Max tried to forget the frustration by indulging in his penchant for adventure. "Man is interested in everything that is remote and unknown, and if he suspects life in any distant point, he is compelled to go there," he wrote in his diary.

In 1859 he left his wife of 19 and went to Brazil, to explore the Amazon and to collect rare specimens. Initially, when he decided to explore Brazil, where his cousin Peter II was reigning, Charlotte decided to go with him, but she got off the ship on the island of Madeira (Portugal) before crossing the Atlantic, apologizing for not being used to the seasickness and storms.

According to one of the couple´s assistants, it was at this point they began to grow distant from each other and stopped sleeping together (McAllen, 2015). Rumors abounded. There had been talk that Maximilian was impotent, that he met a woman in Brazil who'd transmitted a venereal disease to him, and that he constantly engaged in infidelities. Nevertheless, as evidenced by his private correspondence, they were known to have maintained a tender, mutual affection.

When Max returned from his adventure in South America, the work at Miramare was over and he and Charlotte finally moved into their castle on Christmas Eve, 1860. Charlotte spent hours riding, painting, and swimming. It was there where she probably lived her happiest years, although she and her husband craved a higher purpose in life.

Both of them had been brought up to govern. In 1861, they first heard about the possibility of having the throne of Mexico. When Emperor Napoleon III proposed the dangerous undertaking to Maximilian, Charlotte took it with great enthusiasm and interest. "Carlota loved her husband desperately," writes Armando Ayala Anguiano. "The invitation made her delude herself with the idea that the prince's love would flourish again if both crossed the ocean and founded a fairytale kingdom in such a beautiful and rich country like Mexico" (2005).

At Miramare, Maximilian received a formal delegation of eleven Mexican diplomats, who offered them the throne of Mexico. Napoleon´s army had already occupied the Mexican capital. Although the delegation identified with Mexican conservatives who opposed the separation of church and state as well as the expropriation of church property, Maximilian of Hapsburg believed in religious tolerance and separation between politics and religion. He did not believe in the divine right of kings, but in the will of the people. He was convinced that the development of a nation depended on the intellectual and economic potential of the middle class, on educating citizens to be part of a free economy, and that it should all be controlled by the rule of law that should take care of those who remained marginalized (i.e., the poor) (Ratz, 2008). Moreover, in Europe, he had the reputation for being a liberal and a great conciliator, which suggested to many in Mexico, and even to some moderate liberals, that perhaps he was the ideal candidate to put an end to the war.

A depiction of Maximilian and the Mexican delegation

When the delegates showed him proofs of their allegiance and the thousands of signatures from the Mexican citizens (some obtained by force), he heartily accepted the throne and promised to "establish order and wisely liberal institutions, since a well understood liberty is perfectly compatible with the rule of order." Such speech was not precisely what the commission expected to hear. The Archduke´s words alarmed some in the diplomatic mission, but they had gone too far to pull back. Moreover, Maximilian's wife was also eager to go, despite not knowing the real situation in Mexico or the arrangements that had been made behind their backs.[iii] The 23 year old princess was full of hope.

When Maximilian was being offered the throne, it was to replace Benito Juárez, the liberal president who had been unable to repel the French army and had to leave Mexico City with all of the members of his government. The French armed forces may have been more powerful than his, but that did not mean he surrendered. Throughout the Americas, Juárez is recognized as a symbol of resistance against European imperialism, and as a contemporary of Abraham Lincoln, Juárez enjoys a similar veneration to the American president. For many, he's the best head of state the country has ever had, a little David, who with incredible courage and determination, faced the arrogance of the French Goliath and other superpowers of his time. Unfortunately, so much symbolism and exaltation of his virtues have sometimes obscured an objective assessment of his achievements and mistakes.[iv]

Benito Juárez was a pure Mexican Indian, an ethnic Zapotec. He was born in an adobe house in the mountains of distant Oaxaca, in southern Mexico. Like the legendary King David, he was a shepherd as a child. In those years he only spoke in Zapotec, the language of his parents and ancestors, whom he referred to as "Mexico´s original race." When his parents and grandparents died, little Benito was taken care of by an uncle. His brilliant intelligence gained him the protection of a Franciscan priest who urged him to study for priesthood. At that time, it was one of the few ways to get an education and achieve social recognition.

However, the former goat shepherd wouldn´t become a pastor of souls, because the study of theology provoked him into considering it "an immense nuisance." He gave up his priestly career and enrolled in law school, which meant that he needed to be involved in politics. "He was solemn, calculating, prudent, thoughtful, orderly, conciliatory, firm, stern, impenetrable," described historian Enrique Krauze (1994). Juárez became a lawyer, and later a judge and governor of his state, Oaxaca, in the Liberal Party.

Juárez

Because of his political ideas, he was exiled to New Orleans for a while, where he worked in a cigar factory. This is one of the most little known periods of his life. According to some rumors, the soon to be president of Mexico fished his own food from the river and sold the rest in the famous French Market. The hooks he used to catch the fish are kept in one of the museums of that city.[v] During his days in the southern United States, Juárez met other Mexicans exiles, and clarified his ideas to turn Mexico into a Liberal republic, based on a capitalist model in the style of the United States. When the Mexican political landscape changed he returned to his country, and after the Three Year War, he assumed the presidency of the republic. Upon arriving at the National Palace, he realized his problems were far from over. The country was bankrupt, the government debt had accumulated because of the war, and there were guerrillas across the country. The Conservatives had been defeated for the moment, but they were not extinguished; they were merely licking their wounds, planning, reorganizing, and reasoning that maybe the only solution to Mexico's agony was to establish a monarchical regime.

Since he was the president, creditor countries demanded Juárez pay not only his debts, but also the money owed to him by the Conservatives. Being an inflated and unreasonable debt as it was in 1861, he decreed a debt moratorium. It was then that the main creditors, Spain, England, and France, sent their fleets across the Atlantic to see if their cannons were more convincing than diplomatic dispatches.

Chapter 3: Taking the Crown of Mexico

The idea of "turning around" and going back to the old colonial order had been circulating in Mexico for several years. In retrospect, the Colonial Epoch had just come to an end. Mexico had been a subject state of Spain for three hundred years, with relative stability. Since 1823, the young republic, bankrupt and destroyed by its own cannon balls, was fractured by inner warfare.[vi] In 1861 the problem of external debt became critical, and in early 1862, the French army landed on Mexican coasts. It was a wolf in sheep's clothing. Benito Juárez, who had moved north with his government, didn´t have a proper army. He immediately called all young people to join the defense of their country and take up arms in the form of any kind of gun they could handle. Many young men coming out of universities and seminars gathered in the public squares of their cities with weapons (Rivera, 1897). When the French soldiers led by General Charles de Lorencez began to move in, Juárez declared it to be the duty of every adult man to take up a weapon, and declared to award the death penalty to those who lent support to the invaders.

GENERAL CONDE DE LORENCEZ

Charles de Lorencez

In Europe, public opinion was divided. Not even the French were entirely convinced by the hypocritical speech of the emperor, who also had collected signatures of French citizens supporting the "New Conquest of Mexico." "If the Mexican nation remains inert," he urged, "if it does not comprehend that we offer it an unexpected occasion to escape from the abyss, if it does not come and give by its efforts a practical meaning to our aid," he would have no choice but to use all of France's power and crush anyone who stood in his way to the Mexican capital, what the newspapers used to call the Halls of Montezuma.

The French diplomatic agent, Dubois de Saligny, issued an insidious manifesto for the Mexicans, which explained the alleged good intentions of Napoleon. Ironically, he presented the expedition as if it were a sacrifice of the French people: "Mexicans, we have not come here to take a part in your dissensions; we have come to put an end to them. What we wish is to invite all good men to unite in the consolidation of order, the regeneration of your fine country. To give a proof of the sincere spirit of conciliation…we have asked it to accept our aid to establish in Mexico a state of things which will prevent us hereafter from the necessity of organizing these distant expeditions." At the beginning of May, while the French were approaching the city of Puebla, Saligny assured that his country did not for a moment intend to restore old abuses "in such a liberal country like yours."

Dubois de Saligny

In the United States, the French adventure was not viewed without prejudice, not only because everyone saw that Mexico had showed a complete willingness to reach a peaceful solution, but because they considered it to be a blatant European intrusion in their own backyard. "The Emperor of France is a shrewd fabricator of public sentiment," wrote *The New York Times* in February 19, 1862, when the French intentions in Veracruz were more than obvious. "No trickery or falsehood of the Paris Press can alter this fact; no sham plebiscitum, controlled after the fashion of the French and the rebel governments, by bayonets, can satisfy the world that Mexico desires a monarchy, and is ready to accept any nomination the French Emperor may propose. It is not and cannot be made true. And if any doubt exist, it will be very shortly cleared up by the courage and indomitable determination with which the Mexicans will withstand the invaders."

Those would prove to be, to the glory of the southern neighbors, prophetic words. No one could have predicted the outcome of the first clash between the Mexicans and the French which took place on the outskirts of Puebla. The French army was professional, expert in the battlefield, and one of the deadliest in the world. The Mexican army was obsolete and amateurish in comparison. Nonetheless, the date of the battle between one of the most powerful empires in the world and an army formed by students, seminarians, and peasants has been kept in the history of the entire continent.

It was May 5, Cinco de Mayo. A few days earlier, Mexican General Ignacio Zaragoza had distributed the following statement among his troops: "[The French] pretend to give us a foreign sovereign, they look upon us as imbecile persons, easy to be commanded by the force of the bayonet. They are deceived, and forget that against a free people, oppression has no power. Mexico accepts the war; she has not provoked it; but she accepts it honorably. We have new sacrifices to submit to, new fatigues to endure, and new battles to fight; but in presence of the sublime idea of our liberty, nothing ought to daunt us."

Ignacio Zaragoza

At ten o'clock, France sent seven thousand soldiers trained in the Foreign Legion against the Mexican troops. A historian of the time, Niceto Zamacois, who supported the intervention, left a dramatic description of what happened: "The struggle between attackers and Mexicans was terrible. The glorious name that the French have conquered for themselves was not denied in that bloody encounter. Determined to occupy the disputed place, they rushed like lions over their opponents, but with not favorable result, until suddenly besieged with furious impetus by the Mexican cavalry, they retreated, harassed from every point, after two hours of fighting, but willing to return to the assault. After a moment, the French began the onslaught with new fury, and were rejected for a second time. They attacked with an indescribable impetuosity for a third time. It was three o'clock when, having formed a compact column of more than two thousand men, the attackers charged with more courage and resolution over Guadalupe. It was half past four when the French, sad and discouraged, head back to their camp. The joy of the Mexicans was fair: they had fought against truly intrepid soldiers and rejected a tenacious struggle three times. To achieve that, they had shown the same fearlessness." (Rivera, 1897).

Paintings of the battle

At the end of the day, about 500 French troops lay on the battlefield, and Lorencez retreated to Orizaba. "The national arms have been covered with glory," General Zaragoza reported by telegram to Juárez in Mexico City.

Meanwhile, the news of the defeat was catastrophic in France. Napoleon III lost a whole year to regroup and move forward again, at a time that became vital on a geopolitical level. An incredulous and defeated Lorencez issued a proclamation to his soldiers, saying among other things: "You have been deceived like the Emperor, and have been forced to defend yourselves precisely against those who supposedly had sympathy for you. But the deluded France will recognize its error."

With his pride badly wounded, Napoleon III sent a new division to Mexico in October, and increased the French invading army to 30,000 men, of which 8,000 were Mexican adherents, plus an undetermined number of Africans. Almost a year after their defeat, the French attacked

Puebla again, and despite a heroic resistance, took it in March 1863. Given the invader's proximity, Juárez left Mexico City and headed north. In early June, General Forey entered Mexico City. The road was paved for Maximilian and Charlotte, who still believed that the Mexican people, as one, clamored for their presence.

When the French army secured his position in Mexico, Maximilian received the commission at Miramare again, headed by Mexican diplomat José María Gutiérrez de Estrada. Estrada had been one of the first Mexican ambassadors after the consummation of independence, and had an extensive experience in international relations. Maximilian had, indeed, not been the first choice of Mexican monarchists, who had spent years looking for a prince throughout Europe.

When Max and Charlotte welcomed them in Miramare, Estrada must have felt that years of negotiation and effort had finally come to an end. It is agreed that Charlotte had much to do with the decision. Ambitious and aware of her abilities, she wanted to be an empress, but had also had premonitions of disaster. Maximilian said to Estrada that he would accept only if a referendum took place, and it showed that the Mexicans really wanted him as their emperor. With Napoleon III, the Archduke also had lengthy negotiations that were summarized to the following: the Emperor of France would keep his army in Mexico at least for ten years, while Maximilian consolidated his throne and army.

Estrada

The young couple was also visited by a group of Mexican bishops, who told Maximilian how the Church was being dispossessed of its goods, and portrayed Juárez as Satan himself. Maximilian offered to look into the matter once he reached to Mexico. The Archduke, admittedly, did not hear a single version of the facts. He opened the door to other Mexican envoys loyal to President Juárez, who went to Miramare to talk to him at different times about the real situation in Mexico as they saw it: France had entered Mexico by force and the nation considered it an abuse. Diplomat Jesus Terán warned Maximilian not only that it was a lie, but that all Mexicans were waiting for him. He also tried to make him see that the adventure would be dangerous, that he would meet armed resistance, and that his life would be in danger. He also reminded the prince about the legitimacy of Juárez´s government. Maximilian told Terán about the "rectitude and sincerity of his intentions, that a strong and liberal government, with no other aim than justice, was his purpose, that eventually he would conquer all hearts, and would be very glad to shake Mr. Juárez's hand someday." (Ratz, 2008).

Finally, Estrada´s delegation returned with the promised signatures, although it is not yet clear who the signatories were or how they were convinced to sign. True to his word, Maximilian accepted the throne of the ancient Aztecs. In the style of the time, the first to speak was Gutiérrez de Estrada, who assured him that "all the Mexican people, who aspire with unspeakable impatience to possess you, welcome you in their privileged land with a unanimous cry of gratitude and love." Maximilian, who had lost his little kingdom of Lombardy-Venetia and languished in Miramare, saw the offer as a divine gift. Mexico was not a tiny territory on the Adriatic Sea; Mexico would be a great empire, three times larger than his brother's, the Austrian Franz Joseph, who ruled over the second largest empire in Europe after Russia. "I solemnly declare that with the help of the Almighty, I accept from the hands of the Mexican nation the crown she offers me," Maximilian said to the assembly. Days later he was ready to sign the commitments he had acquired with Napoleon III, the real architect of the adventure: "Debts, claims, obligations of the new government, court salaries, and other items in an amount that did not keep the remotest proportion to the real economic state of the country." (Krauze 1994).

To the observer, Napoleon acted like a mercenary with respect to the Treaty of Miramaer. Maximilian's new government should have paid France the cost of the invasion, which was estimated at 270 million Mexican pesos. When Maximilian signed it, he had not the foggiest idea of the actual financial status of the country. The agreement also stated that Mexico should pay France a thousand francs per soldier during the occupation, and France expected the immediate payment of 66 million pesos. There were other ominous signals: the 5th of May, and his brother, Emperor Franz Joseph, making him give up all of his succession rights in Austria. Thus, if the adventure in Mexico failed, he would be left with nothing.

Maximilian hesitated, but Napoleon pressed and told him that he could not let down all of the hopes he had placed in him. They had come too far to repent. England was not convinced either,[vii] but Charlotte, determined, said they should go ahead. "Every crowned head in Europe advised me to accept," Maximilian confessed years later to American General J.B. Magruder, who visited him in Mexico City. "I informed the notables [from Mexico] that if at the end of six months they could bring me proof that I had been elected fairly by the Mexican people, I would accept gladly the position. At the appointed time they came again with the proof, and even then I would not have accepted except to please the Empress."

On April 14, 1864 the couple boarded imperial frigate *Novara*, which already had a reputation for having traveled around the world in a scientific expedition five years earlier. Maximilian had been one of the main sponsors of that expedition, but he had been unable to participate. This was why he'd chosen that boat to cross the ocean to Mexico, to add a little nostalgia and an admission of his wanderlust, since he felt that he was going to wonderful new lands. That morning, many people went to the port of Trieste to bid farewell to the couple, waving hats and handkerchiefs. At the top of Miramare Castle, a Mexican flag billowed from the first sunlight.

At two in the afternoon, Max and Charlotte boarded the *Novara* while cannon shots were fired. Part of their personal entourage, composed of some Mexicans who had been appointed to important positions, accompanied them, as did diplomat Gutiérrez de Estrada. Four days later, they made their first stop. The frigate touched the port of Civitavecchia and the couple took a train to Rome to pay their respects to Pope Pius IX. They attended Mass in the Sistine Chapel, and although Maximilian sat with Pius IX to discuss matters related to the Mexican Church, he subtly sidestepped the issue of the restitution of Church property expropriated by the Juárez government (Ratz, 2008).

Pope Pius IX

Resuming the trip, on April 24 they passed the famous Rock of Gibraltar and headed to

America. "For the first time the emperors, far from their old environment, looked cheerful and carefree. A band of 14 sailors took the mission to amuse and entertain the passengers during the meals," wrote Konrad Ratz, a historian who has produced several books on the Mexican empire. "Charlotte spent time in her cabin, studying books and documents on Mexico, and writing letters. She lacked interest in the beautiful scenery. Only in Martinique did the tropical heat open her eyes to the exotic beauty of the world she was approaching. Maximilian…wrote a manual containing an extensive ceremonial for the court…which shows that he was a laborious man, but foolishly wasted time he should have used for more fundamental matters of governance." (2008).

Near the island of Cuba, after 20 days of sailing, Maximilian allegedly wrote a letter to Benito Juárez expressing his desire to meet him and assuring him that they could reach an agreement. Although the existence of the letter has not been proven, the fact itself would not be strange; on several occasions the young archduke wrote to his political rival (letters which are preserved) asking him, until the end, an opportunity to talk. Juárez never agreed to meet with Maximilian.

Three days later, they watched the snow-capped Pico de Orizaba in the distance, the highest mountain of Mexico, nearly 6,000 meters high. Two days after that they arrived at the port of Veracruz, where dozens of French navy boats swayed on the sea. They still hadn´t conquered the northern part of the country. Hundreds of gunshots were fired to greet the newcomers.

On May 30, early in the morning, Maximilian went outside to the deck of the *Novara*. Before him lay the vast territory that Charles V, a Habsburg like him, had conquered to form the "empire where the sun never set." He descended the stairs and stepped on Mexican soil at nine o'clock in the morning.

Unbeknownst to him, his worst nightmare had begun.

Chapter 4: The Mexican Empire

A 20 peso coin depicting Maximilian

"Mexicans, you have desired me." These were the first, and to some extent, unfortunate words of the proclamation Maximilian issued as soon as he arrived in Veracruz. "Your noble nation, by a spontaneous majority has appointed me to watch henceforward your destinies. I give myself with joy to this calling. Excruciating as it has been to say farewell to my country and family, I did it persuaded that the Almighty has appointed me, through you, to this noble mission and to devote all my strength and heart to the Mexican people that, tired of fighting and disastrous struggles, sincerely desires peace and welfare." Maximilian did not read this aloud before a crowd, first, because there wasn't one; and second, because they decided to stay inside the boat. The soldiers had warned them not to descend to the port to reduce the risk of getting yellow fever, or "black vomit," as the locals called it. They told them that many foreigners had died in Veracruz after just one night in the city. The disease had already claimed hundreds of French lives, as it had 20 years earlier among the Americans during the siege of the city at the height of the Mexican-American War.

The couple walked on the boat deck to catch their first glimpse of Mexico, and they were stunned. Where was the large reception they were used to seeing wherever they went? Next to the houses, churches, and buildings, there was a large cemetery, known as the "tomb of the nations." Napoleon's soldiers had ironically baptized it as "the garden of acclimatization" (McAllen, 2015). Many foreigners who dared to spend the day in Veracruz became infected with yellow fever. Nevertheless, Carlota, now using the Spanish version of her name, wrote home that she was "infinitely pleased with the appearance of Veracruz. It reminds me of Cadiz, but a little more oriental."

The Mexican official delegation came in the afternoon, and several boats were immediately launched toward the frigate. Presentations were made in one of the halls and exalted speeches were delivered. Maximilian introduced his wife, who immediately attracted a great deal of looks from the crowd. In slow but well-articulated Spanish, the Empress thanked everybody, though she was also perplexed by the lack of formality. The next morning, after attending Mass aboard the *Novara*, the couple went to the port, where they were handed the keys to the city on a silver platter, but they were shocked by the nonappearance of the citizens. They took a carriage and traveled through the deserted streets. They saw some welcome arches made with flowers, but not much more.

On their way to Córdoba, the next town, the newcomers first saw the profuse and delightful Mexican nature, and perhaps felt their hopes revived: "Dense forests of beautiful trees: nopal, maguey, biznaga plants and other cactuses; flocks of parrots, hummingbirds and a variety of strange birds; mantles of wild hortensias, orchids, fragrant flowers of glowing colors; rivers and streams of clear water; clouds of butterflies silhouetted against the snow at the Pico de Orizaba and, later, the silhouettes of the Popocatépetl and Iztaccíhuatl volcanoes." (Ayala, 2005). In Orizaba, they attended a party organized in their honor, but they rejoiced in visiting children from different schools, where they showed the patience of the most devoted teachers and gave a coin of gold to each child. In the afternoon, Maximilian visited the prison unannounced, while Carlota attended Mass, incognito, where she had difficulty entering the temple due to all of the women kneeling at the entrance.

"The deserved happiness will shine radiant on the new Empire," the astonished traveler had written in his first proclamation to his new country, and in those early days, observing that exuberance and over 1,500 triumphal arches erected along the way to the Mexico City, he must have seriously believed it. Their journey companions were constantly apologizing for the dilapidated state of the dirt road, which was bumpy and full of holes, but the couple repeatedly assured them they did not care.

The arrival of Napoleon's protégés certainly didn't go unnoticed in the United States. The general sentiment was of skepticism and even a little derision as a result of Maximilian's naiveté. "It cannot be supposed that he has not taken into account the fact that the great mass of the present generation of Mexicans must remain republican in spirit. He also must know that the Monroe doctrine is one of the fixed policies of the United States; that this republic [the USA] will never recognize his rule, and that it will surely, sooner or later, put forth its gigantic power against him."

Halfway to the capital, the couple stopped at Puebla, a more conservative and traditionalist city, where the reception was warmer. Hundreds of people welcomed them from the balconies, while several riders escorted them along the way with their children on horseback. The church bells tolled gleefully. The couple received a new dose of confidence. While in Puebla, Carlota celebrated her 24th birthday, though she was saddened by the miserable state of hospitals and orphanages. Always eager to capture everything in her diary, the empress wrote to the prefect of the city, "The affection, attentions and proofs of sympathy of which I am the object at Puebla, remind me that I am in my new country, in the midst of my own people. Long since united in sympathy with the Mexicans, I am so now with more powerful and sweeter bonds, those of gratitude. It is my desire, Sir, that the poor of this city should share the joy I feel in being amongst you. I therefore send you 7,000 piastres from my private purse. You will devote them to the repairs or the hospitals, the ruinous state of which saddened me yesterday."

For the next part of the journey, Carlota decided to go on horseback. In one of her frequent letters to her family, she expressed her annoyance at the discrimination suffered by the indigenous people: "Nearby all the Indians can read and write, they are in the highest degree intelligent and if the clergy instructed them as they ought, they would be an enlightened race…the epehemeral governments…have never had any root in the Indian population, which is the only one who works and which enables the state to live." Days later, stunned by the inequalities, she wrote, "The level of civilization in this country presents astonishing contrasts," and she expressed her firm desire that, under their rule, Mexico would finally reach peace, something that had been insisted upon in Puebla, a city destroyed by years of civil war. "If ever a country was miraculously saved from a condition out of which it would never have emerged, it is indeed this one."

One year after the French occupation in Mexico City, Maximilian and Carlota made their entry into the capital escorted by an imperial guard. The reception was even more enthusiastic. The church bells echoed the hurrahs and encouragement of the people, half curious and half astonished, who had left their houses to meet the royal couple. All the balconies and roofs were covered with people.

An account of the time described the scene: The Emperor wore a military uniform; his hat that of a Mexican General, and on his breast the ribbon and insignia of a Grand Master of the Order of Guadalupe. The Empress wore a dress of light blue, a blue mantilla, and a bonnet merely adorned with a few flowers. This simplicity was a strong lesson against luxury, and gave a fresh beauty to the natural graces of her countenance, full of kindness and sweetness. Outside the principal gate of the cathedral was an immense arch of natural flowers, all made of red and white pinks, this latter color serving for the inscription: *Xochimilco to its Emperor Maximilian I*. It had been put up by the Indians of that town, and the Emperor expressed a desire to see it again in the capital."

The couple was crowned in the Mexico City Metropolitan Cathedral on April 10, 1864, and the festivities lasted for two weeks. The couple attended most of the parties, trying to win the hearts of the people. Initially they settled in the National Palace, but they didn´t stay long in the building because it was in a sorry state, half destroyed after having spent years without repairs, and plagued by bugs. Maximilian supposedly had to sleep on a billiards table due to the bedbugs. About five miles from the city, they saw the place they were looking for in the Castle of Chapultepec, located on the side of a steep hill. The building had been erected in colonial times by a viceroy named Galves, when Mexico was still New Spain, and its towers rose over the top of ancient trees, some of which had been there since the time of Montezuma. The castle, which had been a military school, and the place of one of the last major battles of the Mexican-American War in 1847, was also abandoned. The walls were corroded, the floor was full of holes, and the doors had been destroyed. Maximilian was ecstatic when he saw it, nevertheless, as the palace reminded him of his beloved Miramar Castle. He decided to restore it and make it their home, on the spot. [viii]

Carlos Martínez Blando's picture of the cathedral

Chapultepec Castle

Tristan Higbee's picture of Maximilian's bedroom at Chapultepec Castle

Maximilian dressed casually, with a wide-brimmed hat that was not very different from the peasants. Sometimes he dressed like a *charro*, especially when he went horseback riding; he wanted to prove that he hadn't come as an unattainable son but as the true emperor of the Mexicans. He appointed some prominent liberals for his cabinet as the administration of the new empire, and he made it clear that his first intention was to create a national army. He also intended was to set the revenue department in order. One of the most pressing issues was the situation with the Church, which expected the emperor to return them their confiscated properties, but Maximilian turned out to be as liberal as Juárez. "The worst thing I found in this country consists of three classes: justice officials, army officers and most of the clergy," he wrote. "The people in cassocks is bad and weak; the vast majority of the country is liberal and calls for progress in the fullest sense of the word."

At the Vatican, Pius IX was disappointed to learn that the emperor had ratified religious freedom and the nationalization of Church property. It's true that the Mexican Church had always shown a great appreciation for worldly goods, but its efforts in education, health, defense of the Indians, and the articulation of society in general, deserved recognition, too. The real predator was the French monarch. During his first year, Maximilian had to borrow to pay the fraudulent claims of England and France, and to reimburse France, Belgium, and Austria for their "military services." In just one year, Maximilian doubled the foreign national debt; he was barely beginning, and his empire was already bankrupt.

From the beginning, Maximilian and Carlota were in the habit of visiting different regions of the country, sometimes on their own. Their intention was to learn, firsthand, the needs of the people, especially in the rural areas. Several historians have recognized that the couple enjoyed high esteem among the indigenous population, which was ironic. Juárez, the archenemy of the Empire, was pure Indian, and Maximilian, a direct descendant of Charles I of Spain, the same king who had allowed the conquest of America which had killed most of the indigenous population. But in the eyes of the Indians, Juárez represented a succession of rulers who had grabbed their lands and been dispossessed of them, a line of presidents whose eternal rivalries and military uprisings led them to destitution. The Indians, perhaps languishing for the patronizing treatment of the royalty, were the most enthusiastic supporters of the couple. The affection was always reciprocal.

For Maximilian, the tours through the country were a chance to satisfy his scientific curiosity. Carlota, much more astute and aware of the needs of a government, had an eminently political objective. In the second year, she visited the Yucatan Peninsula —a lengthy, dangerous and difficult journey—where she dwelled for a time with the Mayan population and took photographs of herself in traditional costume (which have been lost). But her true aim was to make the small countries of Central America gravitate toward Mexico and incorporate them to the Mexican Empire (Diaz, 1976). Naturally, Carlota's visits were limited to regions where there was full French control. Juárez's forces still held some strategic ports and remote areas in the north and south. Mexico was never fully Maximilian's.

Carlota, determined and trained to manage a kingdom since she was a child, participated actively in the government, something that was not seen as right in Mexico. It was considered improper for a woman to make decisions of that magnitude. To her credit, she was the first woman to actively participate in politics in Mexico. Until then, the role of the first ladies was to remain silent, invisible and have children. [ix] According to some testimonies, when she took the reins, things seemed to go better. "If Mexico had ever a president with half the ambition, energy and honesty of the Empress, it would be in a prosperous situation," wrote one of her assistants. Maximilian, on the other hand, was possibly the least-suited man to rule the country. A few decades later, the prestigious *Scribner* magazine reflected on this: "Maximilian was perhaps the very worst practical ruler that could have been selected for Mexico. He was not only unable to see things clearly himself, but equally uncapable of surrounding himself with clear-sighted advisers. The country needed a hard, shrewd, practical soldier ruler. Maximilian was a traditional prince. Charlotte was really the master mind of the two, although only 24 years of age."

The aspirations of the Belgian princess were bold, and her ideas were much ahead of her time in Mexico. With her own hand, she wrote a constitution containing hitherto unimaginable measures: the abolition of work for minors; freedom of religion; the freedom of the press; limited days for the workers with two days off; prohibition of corporal punishment; freedom to choose where to work; obligation of employers to pay in cash (an absolute novelty); compulsory and free school for all children (an idea which the Mexican Liberal Party didn't advocate for until 1906); attraction of foreign scientists and technicians; establishment of a drainage system in the cities; planting trees and the obligation of citizens to take care of them; building hospitals, nursing homes and almshouses; property rights for peasants and peonage release; and granting municipalities their own resources.[x] These measures sought to establish the basis for a liberal but human economic system, in the style of the United States, a kind of proto-social democracy.

Maximilian was optimistic. It seemed to him the French army was unstoppable, taking the last territories from Juárez's hands and forcing him to always retreat farther north in his black chariot, followed by a caravan containing his cabinet and government papers. Juárez issued increasingly harsher laws, condemning anyone who lived in a territory under French control, thus declaring nine out of ten Mexicans as de facto traitors (Ayala, 2005). Juárez was sure he embodied the will of the people, and was prepared to resist in the very limits of Mexico, in Paso del Norte, a border town that now bears his name: Ciudad Juárez. Nevertheless, even when Juárez's cause seemed lost, Maximilan never relented in his intention to have an interview with him, with the intention of forming a joint government.

For the Mexican liberal press, the U.S. and Europe, it was evident that "Napoleon's adventure" was hanging from very fragile wires. It would be sufficient if the French army had to withdraw for unforeseen circumstances in Europe, or if the United States came out of its Civil War and decided to implement the Monroe Doctrine. Add to this the Vatican's displeasure, and especially Juárez's tenacity, since he was apparently willing to prolong the war indefinitely. "Nobody is happy with us," Charlotte wrote in frustration a full year after her arrival in Mexico, already looking at storm clouds on the horizon. "Conservatives, who supported us before, now think Maximilian is too liberal, while liberals call him a tyrant. The French cause daily headaches because they believe the Emperor…does not take into account France's interests. The [Vatican representative] has also been upset with us, and threatens with a rupture with the Holy See if we do not immediately satisfy the claims of the Mexican clergy. Many others who pushed us to this country at Miramar, have not only abandoned us: they prefer the pleasant life of Europe [and] demand lands and substantial compensations from us. We were promised we would find peace upon our arrival, but nothing is further from reality."

"In the evening," writes American scholar Mary McAllen in her excellent book on the Empire, "[Charlotte] sometimes dismissed royal convention and liked to take an Indian dugout, almost alone, out in the quiet waters of the great lakes of Mexico City under the marvelously starry sky. She felt the expanse of these waters. As a royal wife, she compensated for Maximilian´s frivolity and indecisiveness. On some level, Charlotte sensed that Napoleon was about to drastically undermine the Mexican empire and hoped her emperor would begin to face reality" (2015).

Chapter 5: Distress

In 1866, their worst fears began to materialize. France was under increasing pressure in Europe and frustrated with the Mexican adventure. Napoleon decided it was time to withdraw. It was the end of the dream. Furthermore, the Civil War in the United States, which had prevented the country from opposing French intervention, was over at last. The new president, Andrew Johnson, decided he would make his presence felt. To make matters worse, the financial situation of the empire was so desperate that Maximilian confessed to his finance inspector that if Europe did not come to his aid, he would declare bankruptcy and license the troops.

Without a doubt, the decisive factor was the entry of the U.S. in affairs. Lincoln had a debt of honor with Juárez, and Johnson would comply. During the entire American Civil War, Juárez sided with Lincoln; he had granted the United States the right to land troops on Mexico's west coast, where they could march rapidly into Arizona territory if the need arose to confront a possible Confederate drive westward. Now Johnson could return the favor, so in late 1866, the United States sent troops under General Phil Sheridan to help Juárez. The bi-national army began to move southward to conquer territories, and naturally, Napoleon didn´t want to go to war with the United States. Given the situation, Maximilian considered abdicating, but Carlota tenaciously opposed the idea. "Sovereignty is the most sacred duty in the world; one does not abandon the throne as a place under siege by the police. When one accepts a nation's destiny, its risks and dangers are also accepted, and it should never be abandoned. Although we are allowed to play with individuals, in no way can we play with nations, much less should we fail them, because in the end, God will avenge them," she wrote.

During a meeting between Maximilian and his ministers, Carlota surprised everyone by standing up and offering to go to Europe herself, to intercede for her husband. The trip to Veracruz would not only be exhausting; while she was alone in Mexico, in an increasingly hostile territory, she would be in serious danger. Her departure was organized under the utmost secrecy. When General Francois Bazaine found out, he ordered that she not be allowed to leave and sent a boat to capture her, but the princess was faster, and her boat left the waters of Mexico successfully in July 1866. For the Liberals, the news was a sign that the empire was collapsing. In Juárez's army, soldiers cheerfully sang verses that still, a hundred years later, many Mexicans know by heart, possibly without knowing what they mean.

"La nave va en los mares

botando cual pelota.

Adiós, mamá Carlota,

adiós, mi tierno amor.

(The ship is at sea,

bouncing like a ball.

Goodbye, Mama Carlota,

Goodbye, my tender love)"

Bazaine

The Liberals gained momentum. Before the enemy's walls closed around Mexico City, Maximilian's advisers urged him to leave the capital and secure himself in Queretaro, a sheltered city, thanks to General Bazaine, who had fortified it a few years earlier. All the loyal troops gathered in that town, including Prince Felix Salm-Salm, a soldier of fortune who had participated in Prussia, the American Civil War, and now offered his sword in Maximilian's service.

Meanwhile, imperial forces comprised 10,000 men. The Liberal army at Queretaro totaled 25,000, and General Porfirio Díaz was not far in approaching the capital. The siege of Queretaro was directed by the ruthless Mariano Escobedo, a lanky, sharp-faced general who looked even more circumspect with his tiny glasses, elephant ears, and a black beard as spectacular as Maximilian's. The empire had fallen into a trap.

Diaz

As things were tenuous in Mexico, Carlota's journey was pleasant. The princess, who was not aware of the latest news from Mexico, was filled with hope, but her mortification began when she arrived in France and no one was there to receive her. That was to be only her first disappointment. She took a train to Paris, accompanied only by one of her ladies and her doctor, but found no one at the station to greet her there either, and she almost fainted from embarrassment.

They stayed at the Grand Hotel in Paris where she locked herself in her room and refused to eat. When her lady companion entered the room, she found Carlota trembling, "cold as marble." Finally, an invitation from Napoleon III came on the third day. Carlota spent all day crying, but when she got to the Saint-Cloud Castle for lunch, she made an effort to look presentable. She found a very agitated Napoleon, accompanied by his wife, Eugenia. After the usual greetings, the emperor and Carlota locked themselves in so they could have a discussion. "Not a single sound came out of the room for two hours," says an account of the time. "Suddenly, they heard Carlota's voice, screaming: 'How could I have forgotten who I am and who you are? I ought to have remembered that Bourbon blood runs in my veins and not disgraced myself and my race by humiliating myself before a Bonaparte and treating with an adventurer.'"

There was a great silence. Napoleon opened the door, shaking and urgently calling for help. Carlota was swooning. "Please don´t leave me," begged the Empress, but when she was offered a glass of brandy and water, she furiously threw it away. "Murderers, stay away from me. Take your poison away," she shouted, and then she burst into tears. Napoleon returned with a doctor who sent her to her hotel. According to eyewitnesses, when she left the castle, everyone was devastated and crying, even the servants who pretended to have seen nothing. This was the first sign of her madness.

Afterward, she headed to Rome to meet the Pope. Pius IX was perplexed at the broken woman in front of him. Carlota took the cup of coffee he offered and threw it to the floor, screaming that it was poison. "His Holiness watched in amazement how Carlota was convulsing, a flood of words coming out of her mouth in five intermingled languages. Suddenly she said she was afraid that Napoleon and Eugenie had poisoned her, and without delay, she introduced four fingers into her mouth to throw up. When the Pope tried to call Carlota's entourage, she stopped him, and told him softly that they were Mephistopheles's minions from Paris, and they had received orders to kill her as soon as the occasion was propitious." (Vallejo-Nagera, 2007). Carlota refused to leave the Vatican, and days later, she was seen wandering the streets of Rome, washing her hands in the fountains, and mumbling incoherently.

Her brother finally came to her rescue and took her back to Miramare, where she had lived her happiest years. From there she was transferred to Tervuren Castle near Brussels, where she remained for many years until the building was consumed by fire. That night, Charlotte was found wandering through the garden in her evening gown, rubbing her hands, and murmuring: "Oh, my poor castle, my poor castle." In one of her last moments of sanity, she wrote her final letter for her beloved Max: "My dearly beloved treasure. I say goodbye to you. God is calling me. Thank you for the happiness you've always given me. God bless you and make you gain eternal glory. Your faithful Carlota."

Back in Mexico, Queretaro was heroically resisting with 5,000 men against Mariano Escobedo's 35,000, who had mercilessly bombed the city. [xi] Escobedo was consumed by the hatred of everything foreign. "I hope before closing my military career, to see the blood of every foreigner spilt that resides in my country," he wrote to Juárez.

After more than two months of hunger, siege and bombarding, the beleaguered were fed with only horsemeat and mules. They melted the church bells, pipes, and every piece of metal they found with which they made ammunition. Ultimately, it was not Escobedo's cannons that toppled the empire but betrayal, specifically from one of Maximilian's closest men, Miguel Lopez, who had frequently changed loyalties during his military career. Lopez allegedly negotiated with Escobedo to let him take the city in exchange for three thousand pesos of gold.

Escobedo

Lopez

The historical reconstruction of what happened next and the order of the events have been debated for years. After two months of siege, Maximilian's exhausted, hungry, and thirsty troops planned a desperate attempt to break the siege on May 16. Lopez, who was a man that held a position of trust with Maximilian, would lead the column. However, a few days before, he had a secret meeting with Mariano Escobedo in his camp to offer the surrender of the city without bloodshed. Lopez would deceive his troops, and clear the way for the republican army, which would pass through a loophole on the condition that Maximilian would not be immediately captured. [xii] On the 15th, Escobedo's army entered Querétaro through an arrowslit, a column led by Lopez, to take the imperialist headquarters.

Upon learning of the betrayal, Maximilian became furious, took his weapons, and said, "To get out of here or die is the only way." With a handful of men, he headed to a hill known as Cerro de las Campanas (The Hill of the Bells), where he was arrested by Escobedo himself, who triumphantly reported to Juárez that the city had fallen "by force," That wasn't technically true, but Escobedo wasn't going to let a minor detail like that diminish his prestige.

Back in the capital, the Juárez government decreed that Maximilian was to suffer the death penalty by firing squad, despite the fact that the death penalty for political reasons was prohibited in Mexico. Many around the world begged for his life, including ambassadors, heads of state, members of European monarchies, and several prominent Mexicans, and also some who had opposed the Emperor. Even the famous writer Victor Hugo, who had admired Juárez, sent him a letter pleading, "Juárez, make civilization take this huge step. Juárez, abolish the death penalty in all the earth. Let the world see this wondrous thing: the Republic is holding his murderer, an emperor; when that is done, it discovers that he is a man, it lets him go and says: 'You are one of the people, like the others. Go!' This, Juárez, will be your second victory."

Princess Salm-Salm, the wife of the soldier of fortune who had planned Maximilian's escape from prison, traveled to San Luis Potosi where Juárez had been following the whole process. Upon her arrival, she threw herself at his feet and asked for clemency for the prisoner. "It causes me great pain, Madame, to see you like that on your knees," he replied, "but even if every king and queen were in your place, I couldn't spare his life. It isn't me who takes it from him, it is the people and the law who claim his life." Clearly, Juárez understood clemency as a sign of weakness.

As a result, on June 19, 1867, Maximilian and his two highest-ranking generals, Miguel Miramón and Tomas Mejía, were taken to Cerro de las Campanas, the same place where he had been arrested. A few days earlier, they'd informed him, perhaps to increase his pain, that Carlota had died in Europe, which wasn't true. The soldiers improvised an adobe wall on the hill. In the distance, 4,000 Republican soldiers stood and watched in silence as the carriage that brought Maximilian approached. When the emperor saw the hill, he exclaimed: "That's where I thought I would raise the flag of victory, and that is where I am going to die. Life is a comedy!"

Miramón

Mejia

As he climbed, he watched the crowd. A military command had just announced that if someone among the people said anything in the emperor's defense or begged for clemency for the prisoners, he or she would be shot there, too. If anyone uttered a prayer for the prisoners, they certainly did so in silence. Always the poet, Maximilian, watching the clear sky, broke the silence. "What a beautiful view. What a beautiful day to die," he said.

Good-natured until the end, he shook the hands of the firing squad and handed a gold coin to each soldier as a token of forgiveness. His last words were, "I will die for a just cause. I forgive everyone and ask all to forgive me too. My blood will seal the misfortunes of this country. Viva Mexico!" He was shot six times by incompetent soldiers and was thus still alive when he fell to the ground, next to a wooden cross someone had put on his left side. Blood gushed from his mouth as he babbled, possibly asking for a merciful stroke, and a soldier from the platoon approached him and shot him in the heart.

Now the absolute master of the city, Escobedo, still thirsting for revenge, wrote to Juárez: "I have, by the execution of these master traitors, made terror the order of the day everywhere. I have imposed large contributions on the rich, and confiscated their property and their all. I hope to see the blood of every foreigner split."

The Juárez government seized Maximilian's corpse and refused to deliver it to his family with due respect. The body lay naked and clumsily embalmed in the hospital church of San Andrés, Mexico City, where the president and his foreign minister went, incognito, to see him. It was the only time Juárez saw him in person. He examined the corpse for a moment. The only thing that came out of the mouth of the heroic defender of the law, the representative of dignity, the author of great maxims that have been carved in gold, was an unnecessarily insulting remark: "He was a tall man, but he didn´t have a good body. His legs were too long and disproportionate. He had no talent, because although he had a long forehead, it was due to receding hair." The naked body was left hanging upside down from a hook for several days, until finally it was handed over to an Austrian delegation. When the temple became a place of pilgrimage for sentimental masses in honor of Maximilian, Juárez, in a fit of jealousy, ordered it to be demolished. Today there is a statue of Lerdo de Tejada in that place, the man who told the world the details of the unique encounter between Juárez, the living, and Maximilian, the dead.

Chapter 6: Montezuma's Revenge

Days later, the news of Maximilian's death was confirmed in the United States and Europe. Reactions to the news were mixed in the United States. "The murder of Maximilian, which is but one of the scores or murders that mark their [Republican] triumph, bodes ill of the Republican Government of Mexico. There is no hope of lasting peace for a party or government which celebrates so signal a triumph by so signal a crime," said *The New York Times*. Another newspaper, *The Lamoille Newsdealer*, opined otherwise: "To express indignation is a waste of good passion for nothing. The European courts may go into mourning at the fate of Maximilian if they please, for they had hoped that by his means and French bayonets an inauguration of kingly rule would be established in American shores."

In France, the news came the same day that Napoleon III was to present awards at the Great Exhibition of Paris of 1867. When he made his arrival, diplomats and heads of state stood up and left, to his enormous embarrassment. The facts were unprecedented, creating a stir throughout Europe, and marking the possibilities of a new world order. Throughout the Americas, Juárez became a symbolic deterrent of European ambitions. For the United States, unwittingly he became a champion of the Monroe Doctrine. Perhaps that's why the Cinco de Mayo celebration —that first military victory against the French— is more celebrated now in the United States than in Mexico itself.

For historian Brian Hamnett, "Maximilian's execution would be a strong deterrent against European monarchies who pretended to intervene in the affairs of the American republics. The symbolism of an Austrian Habsburg, a descendant of Emperor Charles V, shot on a hill in central Mexico by a squadron of dark mestizo soldiers, did not escape anyone. "The execution cost

Mexico diplomatic relations with several nations in the old continent. It took another president, Porfirio Diaz, to mend the ties with them, including Austria and Belgium. But it is Juárez, from his cold, stone monuments, who, with his laconic expression, keeps repeating his same justification: "I did not kill the man, I killed the idea."

In the wake of Maximilian's execution, nobody told Carlota about Max's death. She locked herself in her room in silence, although she often exploded in long dialogues with imaginary beings, but her words were too disjointed and incoherent to be understood. First she stayed at Bouchout Castle, near Antwerp. She played the piano and listened to music from that new invention called the gramophone, certainly tormented by the fact that she was unable to have a child.[xiii]

In 1875, eight years after leaving Mexico, the mental health of the empress was so significantly impaired that she no longer recognized anyone, not even her brother King Leopold II. When asked how she was, she replied coldly that she was well, and left. She dressed without allowing anyone to help her, took short walks around the park, and sometimes painted. The same year, when she was 35 years old, *The New York Times* reported that although her mental health was in a tailspin, she was more beautiful than ever, saying that her beauty "is now truly shocking." Although she didn´t talk to anyone, sometimes she burst into a monologue of Spanish, German, French, or one of the other languages she spoke fluently, sometimes saying, "*Monsieur*, they say you have taken a wife; a wife, yes, but one who has gone crazy. But if Napoleon had only aided us!" In her later years, she exclaimed, as if to sum up all her life, "Sir, so you have been told that there was a husband, an emperor or king husband. A great marriage, sir, and then, madness. Madness is made of circumstances!" Then she burst into tears.

Carlota's life, one of the most tragic in the history of European monarchies, was finally extinguished early in the morning of January 20, 1927, after 60 years of pain and madness. She had reached the advanced age of 87 and had survived everyone else involved in the drama in Mexico, including Juárez, Maximilian, Leopold, Emperor Franz Joseph, and Napoleon. Even the Austrian Empire had disappeared by the time she died. Her funeral was given full military honors. A small detachment of veterans who had served Maximilian and were still living, led by General Mory, escorted the empress to her final resting place, the church of Laeken, in her hometown. The men placed some flowers on the carriage, and the coffin was covered with the flags of Belgium and Mexico. A heavy blizzard roared outside, but huge crowds defied the cold to follow the empress, baring their heads in the wind, and troops presented arms when the carriage passed by.

Some reports say that, in her last days, the unfortunate Carlota seemed to be coming back from her madness. On one such occasion, she asked the colonel in charge of her guards, "I am entirely free, am I not?" The man, dressed in an impeccable uniform, looked at her for a few seconds and finally replied: "Certainly you are, your Majesty."

Finally, at the very end, it was true.

Online Resources

Other books about Mexico by Charles River Editors

Other books about Emperor Maximilian on Amazon

Bibliography

Ayala Anguiano, Armando, (2005). La epopeya de México, Tomo II. De Juárez al PRI. México: Fondo de Cultura Económica.

Del Paso, Fernando (2009). *News from the Empire*. USA: Dalkey Archive Press

Díaz, Lilia *et al.*, (1976). *Historia General de México. El liberalismo militante.* Vol. 2, México: El Colegio de México.

Habsburgo, Maximilian de (2005), *Máximas mínimas de Maximiliano*. México: Tumbona Ediciones.

Hamnet, Brian (1994). *Juárez*. Essex, England: Longman.

Krauze, Enrique (1994). *Siglo de caudillos. Biografía política de México 1810-1910*. México: Tusquets Editores.

McAllen, M.M. (2015). *Maximilian and Carlota: Europe's Last Empire in Mexico*. USA: Trinity University Press.

Meyer, Jean, (2013). *México en un espejo: testimonio de los franceses de la intervención (1862-1867)*. México: Centro de Estudios Mexicanos y Centroamericanos.

Pani, Erika, (2004). *El Segundo Imperio*. México: Fondo de Cultura Económica-CIDE.

Ratz, Konrad, (2008). *Tras las huellas de un desconocido. Nuevos datos y aspectos de Maximiliano de Habsburgo*. México: Conaculta-INAH-Siglo XXI Editores.

_____, (2005). *Correspondencia inédita entre Maximiliano y Carlota*. México: Fondo de Cultura Económica.

Rivera, Gustín, (1897), *Anales mexicanos; la reforma i el segundo imperio*. Guadalajara, México: Escuela de Artes i Oficios, taller de José Gómez Ugarte.

Vallejo-Nágera, Alejandra, (2007). *Locos de la historia. Rasputin, Luisa Isabel de Orleans, Mesalina y otros personajes egregios*. España: La Esfera de los Libros.

---

i It refers to presidential terms, not persons, since some like Antonio López de Santa Anna were at the presidential chair several times.

ii During his tenure, Napoleon III doubled the area of the French overseas empire in Asia, the Pacific, and Africa.

iii Charlotte was furious during the voyage when she learned that Maximilian had had to give up his inheritance rights in Austria to accept the throne of Mexico.

iv The border city of Ciudad Juárez, Mexico City´s International Airport and literally millions of schools are named after Juárez.

v In memory of those days, since 1965 there is a statue of Benito Juárez in New Orleans, on the corner of Basin and Conti streets. There are also monuments to Juárez in Washington D.C., New York and Chicago.

vi Life in Mexico took place in the capital and its surroundings. People from remote northern and southern territories, Baja California and Yucatan, were barely aware of the coups and presidential changes.

vii Queen Victoria opined that Maximilian would be better on the throne of Greece, which was vacant.

viii The palace, which still stands today surrounded by woods, is the only true castle built in the Americas. Now the National Museum of History in Mexico City, it´s open to visitors. The bedrooms of the Emperors and their furniture are still in their place.

ix Juárez's wife, Margarita Maza had eleven children. Her husband sent her outside the country for the duration of the French occupation. It would take almost a hundred years for another first lady, Amalia Solórzano, the wife of Lázaro Cardenas, to inaugurate the era of first ladies as visible figures of the government.

x It took decades and in some cases more than a century for these measures, which seem normal today, to be implemented in Mexico. The country continued to practice all these vices and even intensified them, at least for half a century. Some of these provisions were never implemented.

xi The rest of Maximilian´s men had left to defend Mexico City.

xii At the end of his life, Lopez, who was always considered a Judas, told German writer Ernst Below that his purpose had been to facilitate the Emperor´s escape, but that Maximilian had stubbornly preferred to fall in the battlefield than running away. Lopez was not taken prisoner when Queretaro fell. He kept his freedom and allegedly received 15 thousand gold pesos.

xiii The lives of Maximilian and Carlota have been surrounded by rumors. One of them says that

Maximilian didn´t die at the Cerro de las Campanas, but escaped to El Salvador, where he ended his life under the name of Justo Armas. Konrad Ratz has convincigly proved this is not the case. Another version says that the body sent to Austria was not his, and that the real corpse was displayed for a long time in circuses and fairs Mexico. This rumor was still in force at the end of the nineteenth century. More insistent is the gossip that the Empress was in a hurry to leave Mexico because she was pregnant, not by Maximilian, but by Belgian colonel named Alfred Van der Smissen. Carlota supposedly gave birth to a son, Maxime, in January 1867. Maxime Weygand himself, officially of unknown parents, served in the French army and fought in both world wars. He died in 1965. He always declined to comment. In 2003 a French journalist claimed to have found evidence that Weygand's father was indeed Van der Smissen, but the mother was a lady-in-waiting to Carlota.

Made in United States
Orlando, FL
04 May 2024

46508740R00029